Your Greatest Asset
by
Tom Leding

TLM Publishing
Tulsa, Oklahoma

The majority of scriptures in this book are from *The King James Version of the Holy Bible* (KJV). Other scriptures are from *The Holy Bible, New International Version* (NIV), (Grand Rapids: The Zondervan Corporation, 1990, copyright 1973, 1978, 1984 by the International Bible Society.) or *The Holy Bible, New King James Version* (NKJV), (Nashville: Thomas Nelson, Inc., copyright 1979, 1980, 1982).

Your Greatest Asset
ISBN 1-890915-05-X
Copyright 1999 by
Tom Leding
TLM Publishing
4412 S. Harvard
Tulsa, OK 74135

Printed in the United States of America
All rights reserved under international Copyright Law.
Contents and/or cover may not be reproduced in whole or in part in any form without the express written consent of the Publisher.

Contents

Foreword v
Preface vii
1 Ideas: Reality or Fantasy? 1
2 How To Choose Your Personality 7
3 Man's Greatest Asset 13
4 No One Has a Totally "Free Will" 19
5 Ignorance Is Not Bliss 25
6 One Who Changed His Personality 31
7 Accept Personal Responsibility 37
8 How To Choose Your Destiny 41
9 Footprints on the Sands of Time 47
10 How To Choose Prosperity 53
11 The Master Key: Choosing Your Words Carefully 61
12 How To Choose Happiness 67
13 Bad Things Happen When Good Men Do Nothing 71
Ten Life-Changing Choices 81
About the Author 83

Foreword

I highly recommend Tom Leding's latest book, *Your Greatest Asset*. A noted author, speaker, and radio personality, Leding showcases man's God-given "inalienable right" in his inimitable style of word pictures.

The right to choose is often underestimated, misunderstood, and misrepresented by various theological and psychological doctrines and theories. Yet it may be the most important principle in life. This is one of those truths that is somehow easy to take for granted or to neglect and misuse.

Often even Christians fall into the apathetical attitude of thinking they have no control over what happens to them. The world calls that fate or *que sera sera*, what will be, will be. Christians can just as easily fall into this pattern of thinking.

Simply because someone feels helpless does not mean he or she is helpless. Leding uses words from wise men down through the centuries to illustrate the biblical truth that, from Adam and Eve on down, men and women have had the ability to control much of what happens in their lives.

Your Greatest Asset illuminates in a clear and positive way that we can take charge of our destinies. Because of God's magnanimous and gracious gift of free choice for mankind, we can make positive changes in all areas of our lives as long as we live.

Your Greatest Asset

My good friend Tom Leding has shown us in this book a fresh approach to the bottom line of positive thinking and motivational teaching. The bottom line is: *Use your greatest asset, the right to choose, to accomplish God's will for your life.*

— Bob Harrison
Tulsa, Oklahoma

Preface

The foundation of my writing and the theme of all my books is Jesus and how to be like Him in living a victorious Christian life. However, the "building blocks" of my radio program, "Who Said That?", and my books are *ideas* expressed in the Bible and in the sayings and writings of wise men and women down through the ages.

Without first an idea, nothing ever happened or will happen.

Ideas precede deeds.

Ideas form behavior.

Ideas cause wars or peace.

Ideas bring prosperity and progress.

The universe with its wondrous stars, planets, and black holes . . . the earth with its marvelous seas, mountains, plants, and animals . . . and mankind with our both terrible and wonderful potential — all originated as ideas in the mind of the Creator. "In the beginning" *all things* were simply ideas, thoughts, and imaginations in the mind of God.

However, ideas that remain simply thoughts in one's mind are not powerful but powerless. The "movers and shakers" in life are those who translate ideas into reality.

In this little book, I hope to make one idea — a fact, or principle, of existence — become real in each reader's life. This fact is that *it is within the God-given abilities of each person to determine his destiny.* Once a person catches hold of the potential and the possibilities of the way God intended for him to live, with the help of God he can make his life what he wants it to be.

I pray that each reader will finish this book a different person, one who knows that God created him or her with one right, one ability, that determines destiny. That ability is the *right to choose.*

I pray that each reader will put this book down determined to examine how he or she has — or has not — exercised this right in the past and how personality, circumstances, and the future can be changed for the better.

I pray that each reader will fully understand how powerful a tool this right to choose is in his or her life, for good or for bad, and will understand that ideas must be acted on to become reality.

Man has free choice — or otherwise counsels, exhortations, commands, prohibitions, rewards, and punishments would be in vain.[1]
— St. Thomas Aquinas
13th Century Theologian

Every time you make a choice, you are turning the central part of you, the part that chooses, into something a little different from what it was before.

And taking your life as a whole, with all your innumerable choices, all your life long, you are slowly turning this central thing into a creature that is in harmony with God, and with other creatures, and with itself, or else into one that is in a state of war.

. . . Each of us at each moment is progressing into the one state or the other.[2]
— C. S. Lewis
Mere Christianity

[1]Aquinas. *Summa Theologica*, Pt. I, First Part, Q 82, Art. 3.
[2](New York: Macmillan Publishing Co., Paperback Edition, 1977)

1
Ideas: Reality or Fantasy?

Great thoughts (ideas) reduced to practice become great acts. . . . Great acts grow out of great occasions, and great occasions spring from great principles, working changes in society; and tearing it up by the roots.[1]

— William Hazlitt
9th Century Essayist

When God said, **Let us make man in our image** (Gen. 1:16), that was an idea. Suppose, however, that He had never spoken that idea forth.

Suppose God had been content to simply think of great ideas? Neither the universe nor mankind ever would have existed. However, God began to *speak forth* His ideas. When He spoke, each idea — from light and darkness to mankind — became reality.

An idea not acted upon will never become reality. Instead, it will remain a daydream, a fantasy that only exists in the mind.

Suppose the founding fathers of this country had not been willing to put their lives on the line to make ideas of freedom and equality a reality? In that case, the United States of America would not exist.

The awesome part of this, as awesome as creation itself, is that the Creator of all things — the One who first imagined all things — included in us the same functions. He created us with imaginations to develop ideas and with wills as triggers to bring those ideas to pass.

Because we are not Him, but "made in His image" — like He is but not as He is — our abilities are not equal in scope or power to the Creator. Nevertheless, in this lifetime, our in-the-image-of-God functions can, and should, operate to change our lives, our lifestyles, and our society.

Because we have wills modeled after the Creator, we have an *inalienable right* to choose how our lives will be. That seems to be man's only God-given inalienable right. If we do not exercise that right, we really cannot blame anyone but ourselves.

Mankind was created with the ability to think, to envision, to have ideas, and to cause those ideas to come into reality on mankind's scale and in the material environment God created for us. Unlike Him, however, we cannot simply and immediately "speak" things into existence.

Augustine of Hippo, noted fourth-century leader of the Early Church who was later canonized by the Roman Catholic Church, once commented on the paradox of a sovereign God who yet allows His followers the right to choose:

> He who created us *without our help* will not save us *without our consent*.[2]

That is a truly amazing fact, is it not? As created beings, of course we are not all-powerful. However, we were given the potential to bring things envisioned into being gradually and over the course of time through the *combination* of our words, our attitudes, and our actions.

Ideas: Reality or Fantasy?

Therefore, when we set our wills *to say, to work, and to act* in such a way that reality in our lives hits the mark of our dreams and ideas, we are living the way God intended His children to live, fulfilling our God-given potential.

You may be wondering where to begin: Does your life need changing in all areas? If so, how do you know which area to deal with first?

Where Do You Begin To Change Your Life?

The first place to start exercising your right to choose is *within yourself*, in your heart. The choice that will turn your life around, if you have not made it already, is to exercise your right to receive Jesus as Savior and Lord. (John 3:3; Rom. 10:9,10.)

After having your inner self, your heart or spirit, changed by God through your choice of Jesus, you will find yourself making new choices about your attitude and behavior.

What about your personality?

What about the "you" that the world knows and sees? Is it like Jesus?

As you study His teachings in the New Testament, you will see how to exercise your right to choose in ways that will cause you to be like Him, to "conform to His likeness." (Rom. 8:29.) That is called "the process of sanctification."

Do you think you were born with the personality you have? Or have you ever thought about it?

No, you were not born exactly "the way you are." Yes, some traits are inherited. However, your personality is the sum total of all the choices you have made since you were a baby about how to act or react to those around you or to things that happened to you. Those choices shaped or caused your present personality to be built on the foundation of inherited characteristics.

For years, the debate has gone on in the social sciences: Which is more important, heredity or environment? Actually, both play a role in who you are. However, your own choices have the most important role in determining your personality.

Do you like the way you are, or are you aware you have personality traits that are negative? You can change. You can choose who you are, because God gave you not only the right to do so, but the ability as well.

How can you change your personality? My friend Jim Stovall, co-founder of the Narrative Television Network, says, "You can change your life by changing your mind." That means changing the way you think, the way you view the world, and certainly, the way you view yourself.

Most people have a problem with thinking less of themselves and their abilities than is true. Others think "more highly of themselves than they ought." (Rom. 12:8.) It is important to be able to evaluate yourself accurately, and it is not easy to do.

Most of us see ourselves as if we looked in a mirror, only seeing what is obvious and two-dimensional. Others know that what shows to others — the "facade" — hides defects and negative things.

Actually, looking at oneself is like going through a Fun House at the fair with various mirrors that distort what we see. Those mirrors are our own or other people's opinions that cause us to see ourselves as malformed or too fat or too thin.

This is why many young women have very good figures, yet see themselves as too fat in the "mirror" of their own minds shaped by the current fashions. Then they develop eating disorders as they try to make themselves fit the "image" in society's distorted mirror.

The biblical way to deal with distortions in the "mirror" of the mind is to *change the mirror*.

Casting down imaginations, and every high thing that exalteth itself against the knowledge of God, and bringing into captivity every thought to the obedience of Christ.

2 Corinthians 10:5

Seeing oneself differently than God sees you is an imagination that "exalts itself against the knowledge of God." It is as wrong and harmful to see yourself as less than God sees you as to see yourself as more than God sees you.

Once you believe you have a fairly clear picture of yourself, you can see what traits need changing to match the image of Jesus and what traits need enhancing and encouraging.

---

[1] Hazlitt, William. "Table Talk" (1821,1822); from *The Great Thoughts*, compiled by George Seldes, (New York: Ballantine Books, 1996, 1985), p. 196.

[2] Draper, Edythe. *Draper's Book of Quotations for the Christian World*, (Wheaton, IL, Tyndale House Publishers, 1992), p. 539.

2
How To Choose Your Personality

Everyone wants to change the world, but only the best wants to change himself.[1]

— Leo Tolstoy
Noted Russian Novelist

If you have read this far, it means you are at least thinking about your right to choose. Perhaps for the first time in your life, the idea of *all* choices being important has become real to you. If so, then you are on the verge of being able to change your life for the better.

Christian businesswoman and author Mary Crowley says:

We are free up to the point of choice, *then the choice controls the chooser.*[2]

Every choice you have made in your life has consequences, and those consequences have exercised some degree of control over you. Making the right choices puts you in the right circumstances with the right consequences.

Perhaps you think that statement is true concerning jobs, marriages, places to live, or vehicles to buy, but wonder how it could apply to your personality? It is true in all areas of life, because the Creator gave us the power to choose in all areas, thus to some extent, we have the power to control our circumstances. We also have the power to shape our own personalities.

Is the result of all your choices — summed up in the way you are now — set in granite? Most people think it is.

"Well, that's just the way I am. I can't help it."

"That" (whatever it is) is *not* the way you were born. It is the way you have chosen to be, and you *can* help being that way.

"My father was that way, and his father before him. It runs in the family" (to be stubborn, to have a temper, to joke and clown instead of facing things, to walk away from differences of opinion rather than participate in quality communication, etc.).

No, you are "that way" because you *chose* to be like your father (or mother), and your parent chose to be like his or her parent. That is "learning from your environment."

In the animal kingdom, it is called "imprinting." If an animal is brought up in a human home like one of the family, it thinks it is a "people," and will act as much as possible like humans.

That animal is "programmed" by its environment and has no ability to change because it had no real right to choose nor the intelligence to choose. The only way it could change would be to be turned loose in the wild and revert to its "natural" instincts, which are hereditary, not learned.

Even then, its destiny would still be determined to a great extent by what it learned while with people. For example, a deer reared by humans would probably have a short life in the wild because it would not be afraid of man.

Unlike animals, man was created in the image of God and given the right to choose. Therefore, once you are an adult, you can change any "imprinting" that happened to you as a child. You have the power to change the way you think, the way you act, and the way you react. As a Christian, we particularly need to pay attention to the "poisoned" imprinting being fed into our personalities through society.

Every day through the news and entertainment media, negative and anti-Christian attitudes, thinking, and behavior is being insidiously fed into our minds. Without realizing it, this immoral, unethical, atheistic climate subtly influences our behavior. By default, the Church gradually is becoming more and more like the world.

When I say "by default," I mean what happens when people do not choose but simply go along with the flow of events. This situation is summed up by what some wise man said about Nazi Germany, *"Bad things happen when good men do nothing."*

To avoid being contaminated by the present post-Christian era American society, we must *choose* not to accept any ideas that are anti-biblical. It is becoming more and more important to remain alert to what is being fed into our minds so that we can choose what to believe, what to hear and see, and what to do.

"Couch potatoes" (those who simply spend hours in front of the TV set without thinking) are allowing their rights to choose to be stolen from them. In other words, they are being "conformed to the world" instead of conformed to the image of Jesus, which is the only way we can achieve God's purpose in giving mankind the "inalienable" right to choose.

What was His main purpose in creating a being with freedom of choice? It was for us to be able to *choose* to love Him as mature children. If we love Him, we will do His will (hear and obey). However, because mankind was given the right to choose, if His creations chose wrongly, as Adam and Eve did, then God was free to make a way of repentance and restoration.

[Apparently, angels were never given the right to choose, because when a third of them chose disobedience, there was no way possible for them to be restored to their original state.]

Most of the things in your personality that need changing will not be accomplished overnight, so do not get discouraged. It took all your life up to this point to establish those traits as part of your personality. Therefore, it will take day by day choices over a period of time to replace them with better ones.

The Choice Is Yours

You can choose to be calm, or you can choose to be excited.

You can choose to trust God, or you can choose to be fearful.

You can choose to be friendly to others no matter how they act to you, or you can choose to have a "chip on your shoulder."

You can choose to be humble and easy to get along with, or you can choose to be stubborn and difficult to handle.

Any of those first options will make your life more successful, bring you more friends, and allow you to be a peaceable person, one more like Jesus. It is your choice!

The true "pursuit of happiness" is the path of the beatitudes. (Matt. 5:3-9.) Blessed are: the humble, those who "mourn" (over unrighteousness), those who are teachable (not stubborn), those who have a great hunger to be more like Jesus, those who are merciful (forgiving and kind), those who are pure in heart, and those who are mediators, or peacemakers. These are your choices!

It would help to get a notebook and make a list of the personality traits you ought — and want — to have. Then make a second list of those traits you know ought to be changed.

Look at your lists at least once a week, and assess whether you have improved. Your personality is no one's responsibility but yours.

The first seven things that Jesus called "blessed" (the Beatitudes) are personality traits and can be achieved only by day to day choices. You must decide whether it is worth it to win small battles over other people — in other words, to "get your own way" — or to win one big battle over your real enemy, the devil. It is your choice!

By beginning with the right ideas of what man is supposed to be (Jesus-like), you can choose day by day to bring those ideas into reality in your own personality. A truly "Christian" personality will have as its root the ideas Jesus taught about the Father and lived out in His own life.

An idea, good or bad, is at the root of all systems — political, educational, philosophical, medical, economic, and scientific — and even all religions.

Ideas are the starting points for bringing what is not into what is. (Rom. 4:17.) Without ideas, nothing happens. Solomon, third king of ancient Israel and reputedly the wisest man who ever lived, wrote:

Without a vision (idea or dream) **the people perish.**
Proverbs 29:18

How do we know that God gave us the *inalienable right* to choose? How do we know that is a valid idea?

How do we know that He not only gave us that right but commanded us to use it?

How do we know that this right to choose gives us great power over our lives?

Let's first find out exactly what an "inalienable right" is and see if "life-liberty-and-the-pursuit-of-happiness" is a right from God never to be taken away (the definition of *inalienable*).

---

[1] Quoted by Dr. Matthew Skariah in *Inspirational Nuggets*, (Roswell, N.M.: World Prayer Band Ministries, Inc. in association with Talking Leaf Publishers, 1993), p. 92.

[2] Quoted by Zig Ziglar in *Top Performance*, written with Jim Savage in 1986 and published with *Secrets of Closing the Sale* (1984). (New York: Galahad Books, BBS Publishing Corp., by arrangement with Fleming H. Revell, a division of Baker Book House, 1997), p. 428.

3
Man's Greatest Asset

You are the possessor of a great and wonderful power. This power, when properly applied, will bring confidence instead of timidity, calmness instead of confusion, poise instead of restlessness, and peace of mind in place of a heartache.[1]

— J. Martin Kohe
Motivational Author

The dictionary definition of an *inalienable right* is "something which cannot be taken away or transferred."

We first find this phrase in American history, not in the Bible. The Declaration of Independence, written in 1776, states that everyone was endowed by the Creator with "certain *inalienable rights*," among them life, liberty, and the pursuit of happiness.

This was one of history's most important turning points. The idea that even ordinary citizens, "the common man," possessed "inalienable rights" where government is concerned was revolutionary. The words and actions of early settlers and colonists in what became the United States combined to create an arrow that has scored a bull's eye on tyranny around the world throughout the past two centuries.

The rights to "life, liberty, and the pursuit of happiness" had not been an actuality in most eras and societies since Adam and Eve were evicted from the Garden east of Eden. (Gen. 3.) Even in America, those rights were never extended to *all* classes and races. On the other hand, in the United States, they have been the rights of the *majority*.

Unfortunately, those so-called inalienable rights are being obscured and confused today. Many born in this country since World War II believe they have a right to happiness, not just a right to *pursue* happiness. Everyone has "rights" which they insist should be fulfilled — but at the expense of everyone else's rights.

At the same time, many rights which the fathers of our country intended that ringing historical phrase to cover are disappearing. For example:

- Unborn babies no longer have the right to live, because their existence conflicts with the mothers' "rights" to have a life free of the responsibility of children. The movement against legal abortion is called *Right to Life* in an attempt to remind everyone of the wording of the Constitution.
- Christians no longer have the right to worship God freely in all places. The rights of the religions of secularism and formerly "pagan" religions predominate in modern American society.

Ideal But Not Biblical

As a matter of fact, as ideal as it was, the phrase coined by the first Congress is not a *biblical right*. After the tragedy in Eden, God never promised man "life, liberty, and the pursuit of happiness" as an *inalienable*, never-to-be-rescinded right.

God promised those things only under certain conditions: hearing and obeying His will. (Deut. 28:1-14.) Those "rights" are not truly rights of mankind, but *blessings* contingent on obedience and faithfulness.

Nor are they "inalienable," for they certainly can be

transferred or taken away. Study the fate of God's Old Testament people, the Israelites of Israel and Judah! (See Isaiah, Jeremiah, Ezekiel, and the Minor Prophets.)

In my study of the Bible, I cannot find that "life, liberty, and the pursuit of happiness" are rights bestowed by God, although they form an ideal that earthly governments ought to strive toward in a fallen world. Neither can I find other "certain inalienable rights" bestowed by the Creator.

However, I do find that God did create man with one "inalienable right": *the right to choose.* We see this first in Genesis 3, where God the Creator gave Adam and Eve the right to choose to obey Him or to obey their enemy, the father of lies and of all sin.

> **And when the woman saw that the tree was good for food, and that it was pleasant to the eyes, and a tree to be desired to make one wise, she** [chose] **took of the fruit thereof, and did eat, and gave also unto her husband with her; and he did** [choose] **to eat.**
>
> **Genesis 3:6**

When God came down and confronted the first couple, He did not evict them from the Garden for choosing, but for choosing *wrongly,* for using the one true right He had given them to *choose against Him.*

Never, since Creation, has God — or will God — transfer or take away mankind's inherent right to choose which He implanted in us. That is an inalienable part of our being. Without the right and ability to choose, we would not be "in His image." (Gen. 1:26.)

In His infinite grace and mercy, God made a way for mankind to come back to Him even after Adam and Eve misused that ability. Each descendant of the first couple may *choose* to be adopted back into His family through His Son

Jesus and spend eternity with the Godhead or *choose* to follow the adversary and spend eternity in the lake of fire.

God gave you *the right to choose*, and He will honor your choices.

You may not like it when He honors your choices, because there always are consequences of making wrong choices. Nevertheless, God will not make choices, good or bad, for any human — even His reborn children. Choosing is our right, which He will not override. Otherwise, He would cause everyone to accept Jesus and be saved. It is not His will that any perish. (2 Pet. 3:9.)

This right, when exercised, is a powerful force in society and in individual lives. For example:

- The result of not being allowed to exercise this right in government results in tyranny.
- The result in not being allowed to exercise this right in public education has resulted in ignorance of God and falsifying of history.

Ever since the Garden of Eden, the one who deceived our first parents has worked constantly to hinder, deceive, or destroy man's one inalienable right. He takes this away from masses of people through totalitarian governmental systems.

He also cheats individuals out of their rights to choose through deception, addictions to various carnal sins, or circumstances that hamper or handicap a person's ideas and will so that he or she cannot freely make the right choices.

Are You Free To Choose?

Are you one of those whose right to choose has been placed in some kind of bondage?

Part of the enemy's tactics of confusion has been to obscure the right to choose by a false definition, "free will." No one really has a "free" will. There are physical boundaries, civil and scientific laws, or consideration of others' rights that provide perimeters for our "wills."

Usually, "chains" around the will are one aspect or another of fear: fear of failure, fear of others' opinions of you, or fear of trying something new or different. "Free to choose" means *free to choose within certain limits*.

The Russian author of several classic novels, Leo Tolstoy, wrote:

> If the will of every man were (literally) free, that is, if each man could act as he pleased, all history would be a series of disconnected incidents.[2]

As one noted teacher in the Body of Christ says, "Don't be flaky!" Use common sense. Exercise your right to choose in times, places, and areas of life where you have the "right" to do so.

God is the only one with a "free" will. He can transcend all natural laws and do whatever He chooses.

---

[1] Kohe, J. Martin. *Your Greatest Power*, (Cleveland: Ralston Publishing Company, 1953), p. 1.
[2] Tolstoy. *Anna Karenina*, Epilogue, Pt. II, Ch. 8.

4
No One Has a Totally "Free Will"

The will, therefore, is not a faculty that one can call free. A free will is an expression absolutely void of sense....[1]

— Voltaire
French Philosopher

Man was not created with a free will. He cannot freely ignore natural or spiritual laws without harm to himself and perhaps to others. If he chooses to ignore or override these laws, unpleasant or even tragic consequences will follow.

We are free to change the way we look by choices of hairstyle, artificial hair color, fashions in clothes, and so forth. However, the right to choose how we look does not include being able to change one's original hair color, one's height, or one's body type. (Jer. 13:28.)

We have the right to choose our president by voting within legal perimeters. We do not have "free will" to actually oust someone from the White House and take over the Oval Office. That is a misuse — mob rule and anarchy — of the God-given right to choose. Other biblical precepts tell us to obey earthly governments.

Man does not have free will to ignore gravity, for example. Furthermore, it is impossible for man to override matter in order to walk through walls or change his shape.

Few people knowingly try to disobey natural laws, although many disobey spiritual laws, ignorant of the fact that it is just as dangerous to do so as to ignore gravity. Ignoring God's laws is a result of ignorance, pride, or presumption. Tragedy waits down the road somewhere for those who do so.

The consequences of this nation's gradual erosion of God's moral laws is that "America has the distinction of being history's most violent "civilized" nation."[2] William J. Bennett, former U.S. secretary of education, says this is the result of "moral poverty."

Unaware of the power of the right to choose, most people turn an asset into a liability by *making the wrong choices* or by not making choices at all. They do not think they can change things.

Of course, you do not get a chance to choose your parents, but from then on, your life is shaped by your choices.

You may say, "But I could not choose where we lived or what kind of lifestyle my family had!"

No, but you chose how you *reacted* to your parents, your brothers and sisters, your teachers, your pastors, and your circumstances.

You chose whether or not to find a way to do better or to live differently when you grew up.

You chose whether or not to judge your parents or caregivers, thus bringing judgment back on yourself. (Matt. 7:1,2.) God never gave man the "right" to judge others. (Using your right to choose negatively in judging others is sin. It will "tie" the behavior you are judging to you so that you are apt to repeat it in your own life.)

You chose whether to forgive or hate, to live in love or in bitterness. (Matt. 22:37-39; Heb. 12:15.)

You chose whether to live in defeat and self-pity or whether to make something of yourself.

You chose whether to believe someone who called you "dumb" or "no good" or to believe that you have potential and possibilities, then finding out as soon as you were old enough what those are.

Your present life is the result of all of your past choices. Can you look at your life as it presently is and see that the exercise of your inalienable right to choose was powerful? You are the sum total of how you have exercised that right.

Perhaps this is a good time to take stock, to do an inventory, to look at all of the times you exercised that right, and to see what has resulted.

Have you used a powerful tool to build a powerless life?

Have you turned an asset into a liability?

Have you been ignorant of the power involved in your choices?

All of those things can change once you see the reality of the wonderful right God has given you. Perhaps you cannot now change some of the consequences of past choices, such as prison or an unhappy marriage. However, you can seek God as to what new choices to make that will improve things and begin to turn your life around.

It Is Seldom Too Late To Change

You have the *right* to turn your life around! To me, this is exciting. You can change an unhappy situation into a happier one by exercising your right to choose your own attitudes. For example, in order for a marriage to work, each party must give up certain other "rights" — those things of self we think the other one owes us — and choose to make the other person happy instead.

Your Greatest Asset

A young minister preached a number of messages recently on how our choices determine our lives. One day, two women in his congregation walked into his study with determined looks on their faces.

When he asked what was the matter, one of them said, "We don't want to hear that 'C' word again!"

He asked, "What?"

With her hands on her hips, the woman said, "We don't want to hear that 'C' word again. You know, *choices*! We're tired of hearing it!"

He had a good laugh — in which they did not join! Then he said, "I'm sorry, but it's not possible for me to preach and not use that word. I can't tell you anything from the Bible or about spiritual living that does not involve the 'C' word."

I believe most of us would be in better mental and emotional health today if we had heard the importance of the 'C' word over and over when we were very small children.

If you are just now realizing the importance of choices and the power they have in your life, then you are ready to make a fresh start. You can:

- Turn poverty into prosperity.
- Turn failure into success.
- Turn fear into confidence.
- Turn a humdrum existence into an exciting adventure.
- Turn depression into peace of mind.

Perhaps you have not realized that your greatest asset is simply the right to make choices. Lack of knowledge concerning anything may be a good and true *reason* for tragedies, pain, and suffering, but it will not allow you to escape the consequences.

No One Has a Totally "Free Will"

Ignorance is never an ideal condition in which to live. I hope the material in this book will bring understanding to dispel ignorance.

---

[1]Voltaire, Francois M. *Philosophical Dictionary* (1764).
[2]Bennett, William J., DiIulio, John J. Jr., and Walters, John P. *Body Count*, (New York: Simon & Schuster, 1996), p. 13.

5
Ignorance Is Not Bliss

Ignorance is not innocence but sin.[1]

— Robert Browning
British Poet (1812-1889)

Most adages or old sayings contain some wisdom. However, the saying, "Ignorance is bliss," is a lie of the devil. God said His people were destroyed for lack of knowledge. (Hos. 4:6.) The early Jewish wisdom writers instructed readers of *Ecclesiasticus* not to be ignorant:

Be not ignorant of any thing in a great matter or a small.[2]

Too many people's lives — even Christians' — have been and are being destroyed for lack of knowledge concerning the one inalienable right God gave them.

This right cannot be exercised, this power cannot be loosed in your life, if you do not know it exists.

Ignorance is not bliss but dangerous, leading to death in one form or another. Most people know in theory that they can make choices, but they do not recognize that fact for the shining jewel, the treasure from God, that it is. They do not value this inalienable right.

Most of us are like the well-to-do farmer who first saw diamonds and became obsessed with how much wealth could be gotten from them. The story goes that he left his children and wife and set out around the world looking for diamonds.

Years later, after he had spent all of his money, he suddenly woke up to the reality that he had chosen to trade happiness and prosperity for an illusion of "a pot of gold at the end of a rainbow." He supposedly died in poverty on the shores of the Bay of Barcelona.

In the meantime, the man who bought Ali Hafed's farm found a stone in the brook where Hafed had watered his cattle. This unusual-looking stone turned out to be a diamond. When more diamonds were soon found, the world-famous Golconda diamond mines in southcentral India were developed.

At least, this is what happened according to the Arab guide who told Russell Conwell, a well-known preacher/author, this story during a trip to Persia earlier in this century.[3]

Whether it is literally true or not, that story is true to human nature and true to the pattern of mankind's history. Its significance lies in the fact that millions of people down through the centuries have spent their lives longing for — and even searching for — the "greener grass" over the fence. In the meantime, they overlooked true riches in their own backyards.

Are You Squandering a Treasure?

In particular, many Christians overlook every day the "true diamond" of their inalienable right to choose. Instead, they spend their lives in vain searches for happiness and prosperity. They make choices, of course, but squander their inheritances as the Prodigal Son did in Scripture. (Luke 15:11-31.) They waste their choices, rendering their ideas powerless.

If you will begin to consider this inalienable right the most powerful thing in your life, you will begin to learn how to use it rightly. As a Christian, exercising this right brought you the most precious thing you have: Christ in you, the hope of glory! (Col. 1:27.)

Ignorance Is Not Bliss

The fascinating thing about God's mercy and about His plan for mankind is that *even those who are not His born again children* have this right. Regardless of whether you are rich or poor, smart or not so smart, male or female, black or white — you were born into this world with this right.

Regardless even of your religious beliefs, you have the inalienable right to choose.

Regardless of your gender, career, social standing, or IQ, you have this right.

Will you squander this treasure from God by simply choosing what color car to buy, what style of clothes to wear, even whom to marry and where to live? All of those things will fall into place if you exercise your choices in order to make your ideas and dreams come true.

Obviously, however, not everything that happens to you is a direct result of your own personal choices. As a famous poet wrote, "No man is an island."[4] You are affected by the choices of your local, state, and federal governing agents, by bankers, lawyers, and doctors. However, many times bad consequences do follow wrong or misguided personal choices.

A young couple chose to make a difficult climb into snow-covered mountains in the Western United States in spite of warnings and even "premonitions" (obviously warnings from God). Then when they got into trouble, and it looked as if they were going to die on that mountain, guess what was their first prayer?

It was not, "God, forgive us for making the wrong choice, for going against the advice of knowledgeable people and even against Your warnings, and please help us out of here!"

No, it was, "God, why did You allow this to happen? Why are You doing this to us?"

It is a good thing God is loving and long-suffering with His people! Help arrived and the couple was rescued, apparently never seeing how sloppy their thinking was and even how almost blasphemous their prayer had been.

Their predicament was the result of wrong choices, as powerful for bad as for good. God "allowed" that to happen because He honors our choices. He will not override the "inalienable right" which He voluntarily and sovereignly gave mankind at Creation.

As illogical as it seems, millions of people are so spiritually ignorant they blame God for the consequences of their own choices.

Is Everything God's Will?

Even some theological doctrines state that God causes everything to happen, thus everything — even wickedness such as Hitler's — is His will. Those people see the sovereignty of God, His absolute power, but they do not see that He voluntarily limited Himself in one area: man's right to choose.

All things that are not God's will are the result of some human being (or human beings) exercising the inalienable right to choose against God's will and ways. Ultimately, however, the destiny of mankind and the universe will come in line with God's will. Everything not lined up with His will is to be destroyed, and everyone who is not in agreement with Him will be confined in an eternal prison. (Rev. 20:10-15.)

If God's will already was being totally done instead of set aside temporarily *by Him* in order for His children to have an opportunity to choose Him and His way *voluntarily*, Jesus would not have taught the disciples "the Lord's prayer." (Matt. 6:9-13.)

Why would He have said to pray for God's "will to be done on earth as it is in Heaven" if it already was being done on earth? If we were puppets, so to speak, God's will would already be done on earth as it is in Heaven. However, we were given the right to choose because God did not want puppets but fully cooperative children.

Some will say, when bad things happen, that those things were "God's will." But were they? Or were they some person's "will" which set in motion bad consequences? You cannot change the choices of others. However, you can change your future by making choices now that will reverse or nullify wrong choices you have made in the past.

After choosing Jesus and becoming a "new creature" in Him (2 Cor. 5:17), the place to begin this process of exercising your right in order to change things in your life is *conforming your personality to the image of Jesus.*

How can you do that? You do it first by finding out from the Bible what Jesus was like, and then making choices to lay aside your old ways of thinking and acting (the old nature inherited from Adam after the fall). Secondly, exercise your right to choose in ways that will develop in you a new personality, or as the Apostle Paul wrote:

> **That ye put off concerning the former conversation** (lifestyle) **the old man which is corrupt according to deceitful lusts; And be renewed in the spirit of your mind; And that ye put on the new man, which after** (like or in the image of) **God is created in righteousness and true holiness.**
>
> **Ephesians 4:22-24**

Your spirit is born again as a gift from God. You cannot earn salvation or do anything to cause it to happen — except choose Jesus through faith. (John 3:3-8,36.) You are saved *by God's grace* (unmerited favor) *through faith.* (Eph. 2:8.)

Your soul, however, or personality (mind, will, emotions) is the product mostly of your past choices. God will not override your inalienable right to choose by sovereignly making you a different personality. You must choose to lay aside or "cast down" those things that are not like Jesus in you.

Becoming like Jesus is the goal set for us in the Bible, and to do that, you must choose to become like Him in attitude, word, and deed.

> **Till we all come in the unity of the faith, and of the knowledge of the Son of God, unto a perfect man, unto the measure of the stature of the fulness of Christ . . . may grow up into him in all things. . . .**
>
> **Ephesians 4:14,16**

For those who think they must be "the way they are" because of someone else's influence, the circumstances of their early lives, and/or the environment in which they live, there is a way out, a door to hope. For a real-life example of one who used his right to choose to transform his personality, take a look at Early American statesman Benjamin Franklin.

---

[1] Browning, Robert. "The Inn Album," *The Oxford Dictionary of Quotations*, (Oxford, England: Oxford University Press, 3rd Ed. with corrections, 1980; first published 1941), p. 101:17.

[2] "Ecclesiasticus" (or "The Wisdom of Sirach"), 5:15. *The Apocrypha*, ed. by Edgar J. Goodspeed, (New York: Vintage Books, copyright 1938 by Goodspeed, 1959 by Random House), p. 233.

[3] Conwell, Russell H. *Acres of Diamonds*, (Old Tappan, N.J.: Fleming H. Revell, 1975).

[4] Donne, John. "Meditation XVII, "The Oxford Dictionary of Quotations," p. 190:20.

6
One Who Changed His Personality

... The arena in which our cultural struggle will ultimately be won or lost is within the human heart.... social regeneration depends on individual citizens living ... lives that reflect the basic and modest character traits ... that the Founding Fathers understood to be the sheet anchor of a free republic.[1]

— William J. Bennett
Former Secretary of Education

Benjamin Franklin changed who he was — an abrasive man who constantly found himself in arguments and contention — to one known for his wisdom. He took for his "motto," or standard of transformation, one I would recommend to anyone as a thought to meditate on each morning:[2]

Finally, brethren, whatsoever things are true, whatsoever things are honest (noble), **whatsoever things are just, whatsoever things are pure, whatsoever things are lovely, whatsoever things are of good report; if there be any virtue, and if there be any praise** (praiseworthy things), **think** (meditate) **on these things.**

Philippians 4:8

The key to Franklin's efforts is the same key you need: *He became aware that his personality needed changing.* As long as you think you are "okay," you will make no effort to be different. I wonder how many people believe they have a great personality and the problem is everyone else? If you are one of those people, you might as well put this book down right now.

This is not one of those "boy, the preacher really got so-and-so this morning" books! It is a message for every reader. How do I know every reader needs to change at least some personality traits? I know that *because we all do*.

Franklin decided that he wanted to conquer "all that either natural inclination, custom, or company" (peer pressure) might lead him into.[3] He was not talking about carnal sins, but about personality traits, such as:

- Not being too talkative
- Being thrifty
- Being sincere
- Keeping your word
- Being diligent to carry out one's duties and fulfil one's responsibilities
- Maintaining a peaceful and calm attitude
- Avoiding extremes
- Not resenting but forgiving things other people do to you.

This is how Benjamin Franklin kept a check on his choices where these things were concerned:

> I made a little book, in which I allotted a page for each of the virtues. I ruled each page with . . . seven columns, one for each day of the week, marking each column with a letter for the day. I crossed these columns with thirteen red lines, marking the beginning of each line with the first letter of one of the virtues; on which line, and in its proper column, I might mark, by a little black spot, every fault I found upon examination to have been committed respecting that virtue on that day.[4]

One Who Changed His Personality

Franklin had some further good advice for friends to whom he recommended this plan. That was not to try to deal with every change all at once. He suggested they do as he had: take one thing at a time and make the day by day choices necessary to transform that negative trait into a positive one. Then start on the next trait that needs changing.

Incidentally, Franklin found that these changes cannot be made solely by will power, although setting one's will to make the right choices is the second step (after recognizing the need to change). The right choices must be made again and again, requiring patience and diligence, along with will power. Last but not least, one must have the help of the Holy Spirit. Franklin wrote:

> Conceiving God to be the fountain of wisdom, I thought it right and necessary to solicit his assistance for obtaining it . . . .[5]

I suggest this pattern: Find what needs to be changed, set your will to do so, pray and commit the result to God, then begin the day by day choices — on one thing at a time. The Holy Spirit will be very happy to help you, because you will be in agreement with His job on earth: bringing us into the perfection of the **measure of the stature of the fulness of Christ** (Eph. 4:13).

Those who do embark on this great adventure of re-making their personalities usually find themselves agreeing with Franklin, who wrote shortly after he began his efforts:

> I was surprised to find myself so much fuller of faults than I had imagined; but I had the satisfaction of seeing them diminish. . . . It may be well my posterity should be informed that to (this plan of changing personality traits by choice), and with the blessing of God, their ancestor owed the constant felicity (happiness) of his life down to his seventy-ninth year, in which this is written.[6] (He lived to be 84.)

The Most Difficult Trait To Change

Franklin found that, although he had success in changing some of his personality traits, there was one that gave him the most trouble of all. That negative trait was *pride*, one of the things God hates (Prov. 6:16) and one which most of us must deal with to one extent or another. He wrote:

> In reality, there is, perhaps, no one of our natural passions so hard to subdue as pride. Disguise it, struggle with it, stifle it, mortify it as much as one pleases, it is still alive and will every now and then peep out and show itself.... For even if I could conceive that I had completely overcome it, I should probably be *proud of my humility*.[7]

Pride is so hard to eradicate because it is not just a trait, but the "root" of a whole family of traits. It may help you to know that there are two basic roots of negative traits: pride and fear. Most of the rest of our negative characteristics are fruit or branches on one of those "trees."

Pride bears the fruit of superiority, arrogance, rebellion or refusal to accept authority, insolence, rudeness, offendedness — even independence, in some forms. The opposite of pride is *humility*. What is humility? David Wilkerson, founder of Teen Challenge and pastor of New York's Times Square Church, says:

> Humility is total dependence on God. It is trusting God to do the right thing at the right time in the right way.... Pride has no patience.... Pride is at the very top of the list of things God hates.[8]

Fear bears the traits of timidity and inferiority, as well as panic and terror or various phobias. An inferiority complex is simply fear of man. The opposite of fear is trust.

The late British Christian author, C. S. Lewis, wrote:

> ... More evil is brought through the desire to be accepted by the crowd than through all the crude temptations of sin.[9]

Keeping track of your choices, right and wrong, on Ben

One Who Changed His Personality

Franklin's "list" is one thing, but I am sure you are wondering how to make those choices. The answer is simple, although it often is hard to do: *Take personal responsibility.*

---

[1]Bennett, et. al. *Body Count*, p. 207.

[2]Franklin, Benjamin. *The Autobiography of Benjamin Franklin*, World's Greatest Literature, Vol. 3, (Reading, PA: The Spencer Press, 1936), p. 102.

[3]Ibid, p. 103.

[4]Ibid, p. 106.

[5]Ibid, p. 108.

[6]Ibid, p. 112.

[7]Ibid, p. 116.

[8]Wilkerson, David. "The Awful Sin of Pride," Message delivered at Times Square Church, 2-8-1988, available from World Challenge, P.O. Box 260, Lindale, TX 75771.

[9]Lewis, C. S. *The Inner Ring*

7
Accept Personal Responsibility

Your past is important, but not as important to your present as the way you see your future.[1]
— Dr. Tony Compolo
Author and Teacher

Many books have been written, particularly in the last two decades, concentrating on *self* — self-esteem, self-affirmation, self, self, self. There is no question one's personality is extremely important, and personality is the expression of self. However, *self* perfected according to the world's present belief — that man is his own god — is quite different from *self conformed to the image of Jesus.*

The New Age movement crystallized this self-focus, beginning in the 60s, and, combined with modern psychology, has developed a religion centered around the environment. The New Age "propaganda" being disseminated throughout our culture today is that man is simply the highest animal on the evolutionary chain. They believe that all mankind's problems are the fault of the Judaeo-Christian heritage of our ancestors.

Modern psychology claims your parents are the cause of all your personality problems, and their parents caused theirs, *ad infinitum* — all going back to Christianity. In reality, this is "blame shifting."

> The New Age Movement magnifies self and encourages its followers to foster a worship of self, apart from the worship of

the Creator. This . . . combination of Eastern religion and Western philosophy. . . . puts self on a pedestal. From the beginning of time, man has rebelled against the worship of God, and created various images of worship to make himself feel good.[2]

Actually, the elevation of man to "godhood" and the excuse of blaming someone else for your own choices began in the Garden of Eden. Satan tempted Adam and Eve with the idea of becoming like God, and when the consequences of their choices began to control their destinies, both Adam and Eve "blame-shifted." Adam blamed her, and she blamed the devil. The *cause* of the fallen world in which we have lived since then, however, is the result of only one thing: *the choices of Adam and Eve.*

They did not have to believe Satan's lies or choose his way. No force was involved. The devil simply offered them an *idea* that destroyed them and has affected everyone on earth ever since. Poverty, sickness, sin, evil, and death are the *consequences* of their choices.

While we have to live in a world which reflects the consequences of their choices, we cannot blame *our* personal problems on *their* choices. We will be required by God to answer for our own choices, just as Adam and Eve had to take the responsibility for theirs.

Motivational speaker and author Zig Ziglar wrote:

> If you are the way you are because of someone else, then here's what you do. Take the person who's responsible for the way you are to the psychologist, the psychologist will treat him or her, and you will get better! See how crazy that is? If you break your arm, you don't send . . . the one who pushed you (to the doctor). You go yourself.[3]

It is a waste of time to blame someone else. Put that time and energy into fixing the problem. Choose to change the negative things in your life, starting with your personality. This is not an easy project, but the success of "life, liberty, and pursuit of happiness" depends on the kind of personality you have.

How To Change Negative Traits

To change any trait, *choose to do the opposite* from what your present inclination is to do. For example:

- If you have a problem with not wanting to be told what to do (sometimes called "self-will"), then make yourself do whatever it is you are told to do — unless it is harmful to yourself or someone else or is against biblical principles.

  - If your personality trait that needs changing is pride masquerading as independence, choose to accept anything or any help offered you. You may even have to choose to ask for help in order to break that trait.

Have you ever refused help out of pride, then wondered why God did not answer prayer? God cannot bless a prideful person with goods, friends, or anything else. That person instead of being thankful would be offended.

How did Franklin know he had pride? He knew because a friend to whom he related his attempts to change his personality told him so! A real friend is one who will tell you the truth about yourself in a loving way. If you cannot immediately recognize what needs changing in your personality, I hope you have some true friends whom you can trust.

> A Quaker friend . . . kindly informed me that I was generally thought proud, that my pride showed itself frequently in conversation, that I . . . was overbearing and rather insolent, not content with being in the right when discussing any point.[4]

In spite of his rueful words indicating that he had not been able to change pride, Franklin did try diligently to conquer this trait by choosing to do the opposite and had some degree of success:

> I made it a rule to forbear all direct contradiction to the sentiments of others and all positive assertion of my own. I even forbade myself . . . the use of every word or expression in the language that implied a fixed opinion. . . . When another asserted something I thought was an error, I denied myself the pleasure of contradicting him abruptly . . . (instead) I began my answer by observing that in certain cases . . . his opinion would be right, but that in the present case there *appeared or seemed to me* some difference.[5]

This revered elder statesman wrote that he soon found his conversations with others more pleasant and that his new modest approach made people more ready to listen to his opinions. He also found he was not as likely to be embarrassed when he was in the wrong! In addition, his humbler attitude made it easier to persuade others they were wrong in the instances when he *was* right.

He found before long that his relationships improved immensely. Why? It was because he had exercised his right to choose to make a real difference in his personality. He chose to speak and act with humility.

If you will take personal responsibility for your personality and make the decision to exercise your right to choose to change those things that ought to be changed, I promise you that will change your destiny.

---

[1] Quoted in Ziglar's *Top Performance*, p. 431.
[2] Skariah, p. 69.
[3] Ziglar. *Top Performance*, pp. 430, 431.
[4] Franklin, p. 114.
[5] Ibid, p. 115.

8
How To Choose Your Destiny

Many people are reluctant to make the one quality decision that will change their lives because they don't really believe they have a choice. I'm here to tell you that you do have a choice.[1]

— Jim Stovall
Co-founder, President
Narrative Television Network

What is *destiny*? The dictionary has three definitions:

1) the seemingly inevitable or necessary succession of events, 2) what will necessarily happen to any person or thing (one's fate), 3) that which determines events . . . .[2]

Those are all man's definitions and usually thought of in the sense of some supernatural cause or being who controls what happens to us. However, the third definition is closer to biblical terms: *that which determines events.*

God created everything perfect. (Gen. 1:31.) In order to have children who would choose to love Him and choose to be like Him, as we have seen in the above chapters based on Scripture, He left room for man's choices to bring imperfection into the universe. Therefore "that which determined today's events" in your life includes five sets of choices:

    1. Adam and Eve's choices

    2. Collective choices of everyone who has since lived

    3. Choices of your direct ancestors and parents

4. Choices of authorities over you, including teachers, bosses, governments, etc.

5. Choices made by you in your own lifetime

Obviously, you cannot do anything about the first four sets of choices. However, within the conditions of your life determined by the first four sets of choices, there is great latitude left for you to greatly affect and direct your destiny.

Let's look at a hypothetical example:

Suppose you are a black man whose ancestors were brought to this country in slavery or a white man whose ancestors were brought to this country as indentured servants. Suppose your parents were poor Southern sharecroppers. None of those things were by your choice nor can they be changed. However, *your* personal destiny *is* still yours to choose.

Do you have to remain a poor sharecropper? No.

In public school, did you choose to learn or to run with the crowd?

Did you choose to get further education through working your way or through grants?

Have you made an effort to find where your abilities lie?

Have you sought the Lord for an idea or dream for your life?

Have you, or will you, re-shape your personality, change wrong attitudes, habits, and behavior, and set your will to achieve the highest destiny possible?

If you are one who needs encouragement, who needs to be strengthened in your belief that things can be different, that you can do whatever you set your will to do, then spend time studying the lives of leaders in every field. This is what I did. In some of my previous books, I have presented stories about leaders whose lives impressed me because of their patience, diligence, and determination to succeed.[3]

A few of those who began in poverty or unfortunate circumstances are Benjamin Franklin, Abraham Lincoln, George Washington Carver, inventors such as Thomas Edison, and even President Clinton. Whether you agree with his policies or not, his life is an example of someone who dreamed a dream as a teenager of becoming President of the United States. Then he set his will and made choices one after another until he achieved that destiny.

He came from a broken home and a poor environment, but he chose to study hard and to tenaciously take every opportunity in education and politics that would get him to the fulfillment of his dream.

A prayer by the Roman Catholic saint, Francis of Assisi, can be summed up like this: Change the things that can be changed, and leave up to God the things you cannot change.

Choose To Believe It Is Up To You

I once read a story about a man during the Depression who wondered why one butcher shop near him was thriving, while another nearby was going broke. In pre-supermarket days, people bought meat one place, fresh vegetables another, and dairy products from a delivery wagon or truck.

This man wondered, "Why are people buying from one butcher but not from the other? Does one have better meat to offer?"[4]

He bought from both stores and found the economic climate was the same, the neighborhood was the same, the stores looked alike, the product was the same, and the patrons were the same people. What was the factor that made the difference between success and failure?

After visiting both stores to buy meat, he found why one store owner was making money in spite of hard times, while it seemed "hard times" had come to live at the other store. The difference was in the *choices* both butchers were making as to how they reacted to hard times.

The butcher who was going broke chose:

— to believe that circumstances controlled his destiny

— to carry a "chip on his shoulder" because life was "not being fair to him"

— to accept the "fate" others' choices seemed to have brought upon him.

He was impolite and short with customers, because of feeling sorry for himself. He made no effort to clean up his shop or to encourage customers to come to him. He tried to force customers to take the meats he wanted to sell instead of the ones they wanted to buy.

The other butcher was totally different. He chose:

— to believe that he was in charge of his success, not circumstances

— to be courteous and helpful

— to understand that the customers — or the world — did not owe him anything, but that he owed them good service.

He made his shop inviting, made people feel good about visiting him, and worked hard to satisfy their needs, not his own.

The man who noticed the difference in the two shops and found out what caused it also made a choice. *He chose to believe it was up to him* whether he made it in life or not, even in the midst of the Depression. It was not the government, or the economy, or bad customers — his destiny depended on his choices.

Do you want to get ahead on your job? Make some quality choices:

- Get to work on time, or even a few minutes early
- Do the work the very best you know how
- Put in all the time for which you are paid
- Look for ways the job can be improved
- Learn all you can about the work you are doing
- Choose to keep a good, pleasant attitude to other employees as well as to those in authority.
- Remember to do the work as "unto the Lord"

If you will not do a good job for a mere man or a faceless company, how will you ever be a good, faithful worker in whatever God wants you to do?

Many people have started their climb to success during hard times simply because they did not believe that outward circumstances controlled their destinies. Nor did they believe that it was God's will for them to be poor and unhappy.

In the next chapter, I want to give you some examples of people whose choices not only made a difference in *their* destinies but in *our* everyday lives, as well.

---

[1] Jim Stovall. *You Don't Have To Be Blind To See*, (Nashville: Thomas Nelson, Inc., Publishers, 1996), p. 32

[2] *Webster's New World Dictionary*, Third College Edition, (New York: Simon & Schuster, Inc., 1994, 1991, 1988), p. 374.

[3] *Who Said That?, Rags to Riches: You Don't Have To Be Poor, The Making of a King*, (Tulsa: TLM Publishing, 1996, 1997).

[4] Kohe, pp. 27-29.

9
Footprints on the Sands of Time

*Lives of great men all remind us
We can make our lives sublime,
And, departing, leave behind us,
Footprints on the sands of time.*[1]

— Henry Wadsworth Longfellow
19th Century American Poet

Longfellow's poem, "A Psalm of Life," from which we get the phrase "footprints on the sands of time" was written at a low point in his life. He called the poem, "a voice from my inmost heart at a time when I was rallying from depression."[2]

This famous poet exercised his right to choose and kept his destiny on track, instead of letting his mental and emotional state dictate depression and failure. He chose to use his inspirational talent to not only help himself but to help others.

Jim Stovall, whom I have quoted a couple of times, had one of the best opportunities I know of to let circumstances determine his destiny. No one would have blamed him if he decided that he could not exercise his right to choose. However, Jim would not let anything or anyone keep him from exercising his inalienable right from God.

As a teenager undergoing a routine physical for college entrance, Jim's doctor discovered he had a degenerative eye disease that would cause complete blindness within about 10 years. Jim had known since the age of seven that he had a vision problem, but had no idea that, eventually, he would be blind.

He battled the three "Big D's" as strongly as he had fought opponents in the high school wrestling ring. What were his three big opponents? Despair, discouragement, and defeat. How did he beat them? He did it by continuing to work toward goals in football and wrestling. He lost a sports scholarship but won a gold medal in national championships even after he was unable to see as far in front of him as the judges' stand.

During the years his eyesight was failing but not yet gone, he spent time with government agencies set up to help the blind. He visited a sheltered workshop where a social worker told him blind people were trained in work that would help them become self-sufficient.

He found that this "wonderful" training was how to sit at a table all day and make brooms or put erasers on the ends of pencils. In his autobiography, he wrote:

> (That visit) told me the government's "dream" for my life. It wasn't a good-enough dream. I feel quite certain it isn't a good-enough dream for most of the people in that sheltered workshop. . . . Someone told them that was the most they could *expect* from their lives, and they bought into that expectation.[3]

In the book about his life, *You Don't Have To Be Blind To See*, Jim tells of the years he spent working toward a personally fulfilling goal. He exercised his right to choose in one way after another that took him farther toward that goal. He and his wife spent several years as very successful stockbrokers, then he and a partner invented narrative television.

He did it with the help of people who *did not know it could not be done*, as all the "experts" said. Now his network is international and in millions of homes. Those who cannot see the screen can hear a narration of the action taking place as well as the dialogue of the actors.

Jim's experience reveals the fact that an integral part of success is the *expectation of success*. If you make a choice and expect it not to work, then your choice has been wasted.

We hear often about the success of famous inventors, athletes such as the newest sensation, golfer Tiger Woods, and world leaders, many of whom started in poverty, were uneducated, and failed more than once before making it. They are great examples for the rest of us. They give us hope and role models to follow.

Footprints Without Fame

However, what about those who achieve success, but not fame? Perhaps you have an idea that would satisfy you. "Building a better mousetrap" does not always bring the world to your door. However, it does bring a sense of a job well-done and a goal accomplished.

For example, Levi Hutchins, who lived in New Hampshire in 1787, invented the alarm clock. He never made any money from it nor did he become famous. However, he died satisfied at achieving his goal: to develop a way not to oversleep. He needed to get up at 4 a.m. to be at his job on time.[4]

The moral of Levi Hutchins is: Do not sell yourself short. Do not set too small a goal for yourself. You can achieve what you choose.

Many small items that we take for granted today were the end result of someone's ambition, someone's choice of how to make an idea a practical reality. Things such as the pencil with eraser, chewing gum, the ice cream cone, shoelaces, toothbrushes, *ad infinitum*.[5] All were developed as recently as the 19th century.

No idea is too small to become a force in your life. Where would we be without safety pins, paper clips, bobby pins, zippers, and toilet paper? How did the millions of people manage without all of these small items we take for granted? Can you imagine the world without toilet paper before 1857?

No matter how good your idea is, you will never make footprints on the sands of time (with or without fame and fortune) unless you bring that idea into the realm of reality.

Even good friends and family members can discourage you from proceeding, although their intentions are good.

Walter Hunt, a New York Quaker who invented the safety pin, also invented the repeating rifle, a nail-making machine, an ice plow, and other things, as well as a sewing machine (in 1832). He sold his idea for the safety pin for $400, because he needed $15 to pay a debt, and never received another penny out of it.

Hunt is another example not to follow, although he left footprints on the sands of time. He was short-sighted and prosperity apparently was not one of his goals. He dropped the idea of the sewing machine because his daughter convinced him it would put too many seamstresses out of work![6]

Ideas never worked out are simply fantasies.

Do you want the world to beat a path to your door?

Do you want personal satisfaction?

Do you want prosperity?

Begin to make the choices that will achieve those goals.

Nineteenth-century essayist Ralph Waldo Emerson is

credited with putting the "mousetrap concept" into words in a lecture in San Francisco:

> If a man can write a better book, preach a better sermon, or make a better mousetrap, than his neighbor, though he builds his house in the woods, the world will make a beaten path to his door.[7]

Dear Mr. Emerson: It works for me!

In the next chapter, we will look at some other ways you can be hindered from developing your ideas and reaching your goals.

---

[1]Longfellow, Henry Wadsworth, "A Psalm of Life," *A Book of American Literature*, (New York: The MacMillan Company, 1946 ed., orig. pub. 1927), p. 586.

[2]Ibid.

[3]Stovall, p. 103.

[4]Wallechinsky, David and Wallace, Irving. *The People's Almanac*, (Garden City, N.Y.: Doubleday & Company, Inc., 1975), p. 910.

[5]Ibid, pp. 910-915.

[6]Ibid, p. 914.

[7]Ibid, p. 910.

10
How To Choose Prosperity

*If you are fearful of what tomorrow may be,
If you are willing to forever be free,
Then you need to take hold of your life from
this day,
And you must plan a far better way.*[1]

— Peter J. Daniels
Australian Motivational
Speaker and Writer

One thing anyone who has made a financial success will tell you is that *if you do not change your thinking, you will not change your financial status.* You must choose against a poverty mentality and take on a prosperity mentality.

The first step in choosing prosperity is to believe two things: 1) It is God's will for you, and 2) it is possible for you.

How can you know that it is God's will for you to prosper? We can know this from His Word, in which He also tells us how to prosper.

> **Blessed is the man that feareth the Lord, that delighteth greatly in His commandments ... Wealth and riches shall be in his house: and his righteousness endureth for ever.**
>
> **Psalm 112:1,3**

In other places the Lord shows us that "fearing" Him means obeying Him. Poverty was part of the curse about which the people of Israel were warned in Leviticus 26 and Deuteronomy 28. Hearing God's commandments and obeying them puts you in a place where prosperity can flow in your life. (Isa. 1:19.)

You can see that making a choice to be prosperous is not enough. It must be preceded by choosing to believe God's Word and choosing to believe in yourself. Which brings us to the question, *What is prosperity?*

The Bible tells us what prosperity means in 3 John 2:

Beloved, I wish above all things that thou mayest prosper and *be in health*, even as thy soul prospereth.

What is your soul? It is your mind, your will, and your emotions – that part of you that we call "your personality." Benjamin Franklin plainly wrote that fame, money, and political power were not enough to bring him contentment, as long as his soul was discontented. Without peace of mind, no one prospers.

You must take hold of your life in order to have any hope of changing your situation and circumstances. How do you "take hold of your life"? How can you make certain that your plans for "a far better way" can be carried out?

Daniels' verse about goals continues with the answer:

> Then chase after your goal with a desperate desire,
> With passion and excellence, as if you were on fire.
> Do not be timid or reluctant or slow,
> Just move into top gear and let all systems go.[2]

If you have not set a goal for your life, then it is time that you did. Seek the Lord until you "know that you know" what His goal is for you in life. The goal may not be in ministry, but in business or entertainment or other fields of endeavor. In addition, you need goals for your present employment, as well as for your personal and spiritual development.

Once you have a goal or goals settled firmly in your mind, begin to exercise your right to choose by taking step after step toward that goal — just as President Clinton did.

Has the fact that your choices can determine your destiny hit you like a thunderbolt out of the blue? (I hope it has.) Then you are ready to embark on the journey toward fulfilling what has to be your first goal, your first step toward prosperity. That, of course, is re-shaping your personality.

When you have tried Franklin's method of charting such changes, you will begin to feel much more peace of mind. You will find that you get along with people much easier. Getting along with other people, "doing to others as you would have them do to you," is a big move toward success, contentment, and prosperity.

Once you feel comfortable being "a different person," you can begin to take charge of your destiny by setting a goal for your life, one that involves prosperity.

Do You Think "Poor"?

Few goals can be accomplished in terms of job, career, profession, ministry, or politics without money. Therefore, prosperity cannot be totally focused on money but neither can there be prosperity without money.

A "poverty mentality" means "thinking poor," "talking poor-mouthed," and believing you "will never have anything." You will never prosper until you exercise your right to choose and throw out that thinking in favor of a prosperity mindset.

Throw out all of those ideas that you have to be poor, and replace them with the idea that *you can prosper*. Poverty is not a virtue, nor does it bring humility. Poverty brings humiliation, embarrassment, and degradation. None of that is of God, nor is it His will for His children.

By giving us the right to choose, He made a way for each of us to achieve prosperity in our lives. He will help us if we ask Him for ideas as to how to prosper, but He will not shower gold on us from Heaven. He also expects us to work diligently. As an example, He worked six days and only rested one in creating the earth.

If you want God to help you achieve prosperity, then your motives must be right. True prosperity — spirit, soul, and body — only comes to those who seek wealth without greed, covetousness, or for itself, which is called miserliness.

Remember the old story about King Midas, whose touch turned everything to gold? When everything around him, including his beloved little daughter, was solid gold, he found gold was not truly prosperity after all.

Prosperity must be a means to an end, not an end in itself.

Prosperity is having abundance, enough for yourself and to give away.

Prosperity will not come to Christians who love money, but to those who love what they can do for God and for others with money. The Apostle Paul did not write that money is evil, but that "the love of money" (greed, avarice, covetousness) is "the root of all evil." (1 Tim. 6:10.)

Think of that! *All crime, wars, and hardships stem from people's love of money.*

Millions of people would like to be prosperous, usually defining that condition in terms of money. However, many wealthy people are not prosperous in health, mental or physical. They are not prosperous and happy in their relationships, nor are they prosperous spiritually.

Here are ten steps to true prosperity.

Ten Steps to Prosperity

1. *Choose a prosperity mindset.* You will never achieve prosperity in any area as long as you "think poor."

2. *Desire to reach the goal of prosperity with all your heart.*

Daniels, whom I quoted at the beginning of this chapter, is a member of Robert Schuller's International Board of Directors of the Crystal Cathedral Ministries. He has lectured around the world on how to reach your life's goals and wrote this concerning desire and motives:

> Desire is the emotional thrust resulting from strong compulsive motives. So *the clearer the motive, the stronger the desire.* . . . It is of paramount importance to have clarity of thought at the motive level.[3]

3. *Care about your goal passionately.*

It is not enough to desire strongly to win the race. The minute you stop caring about reaching your goal, the minute you lose "your first love" for anything (Rev. 2:4), you are on the way to being defeated, no matter how much you may desire to win. You must care passionately enough about the race itself not to let yourself be hindered.

4. *Deal with hindering attitudes.* Three hindering attitudes Daniels mentioned in his poem will prevent you from even starting toward your goal: timidity, reluctance to do what is necessary, and moving too slowly. Three attitudes that hinder you after you start toward your goal are complacency, apathy, and fear of failure. Any of those will sap your determination to win.

5. *Choose to seek prosperity with the right motives:* for the sake of the Kingdom of God, your family, and to help others.

6. *Make whatever preparations are necessary.* Study whatever field or area you have chosen in which to seek

prosperity. Learn everything you possibly can about your goal and how other people have accomplished their goals.

7. *Carry out each step with excellence*; in other words, do everything along the way the best you possibly can.

8. *Choose good thoughts, spiritually healthy thoughts, about wealth.* Eliminate thoughts like the following from your mind, and more importantly, refrain from expressing them verbally:

- "I can't afford that."
- "I'm never going to have anything."
- "Everything bad always happens to me."

Instead of empowering a poverty mentality, speak the same facts optimistically:

- "The funds are not available right now, but I will buy that soon."
- "I am going to have everything that I need and more. I have a Father who wants me to prosper, and He owns everything."
- "I have bad times, like everyone else, but I also have just as many or more good times."

When one man married, he said, "My wife and I cannot take a honeymoon right now, but we are going to Europe for our honeymoon."

Twenty years later, they went. If he had begun to think and to say they would love to go but could not afford it, he probably would have continued to think and speak that way. The result would be that they would never have gone to Europe.

During those years, they never lost the hope, the expectation, and the determination to reach the goal of Europe.

9. *Choose to measure your life by goals achieved.*

Do you measure your life in terms of time — days, weeks, months, and years? Or do you measure your life by accomplishments?

The calendar is not your god. Neither is the clock. Both will disappear one day, and your main concern then before the Lord will be if you used time to the best advantage. Prosperity is using the time given you rightly, just as you would use money in a right way.

Do not ever forget that you have power to direct your life as you want it to go in spite of circumstances. That "power" is your right to choose.

10. *Never lose hope of reaching your goal.*

Hope is the climate in which right choices are made. There are three things, however, that will destroy hope: speaking negatively, feeling self-pity, and not setting goals.

- Without hope, there are no ideas, dreams, and goals.
- Without ideas, nothing happens.
- Without goals, ideas never become reality.

The Rev. Charles Swindoll says that hope is as important to us "as water to a fish" and as vital to our well-being as "electricity is to a light bulb." In other words, we will not get very far without it.[4]

Once you have taken all those steps, perhaps the most important thing you can do to reinforce your choices, to buttress your ideas, and to keep you on track toward your goals is to *watch the words you speak.*

---

[1]Daniels, Peter J. *How To Reach Your Life Goals*, (Tulsa: Honor Books, 1995), p. 7.
[2]Ibid.
[3]Ibid, p. 19.
[4]Swindoll, Charles R. *Hope Again*, (Dallas: Word Publishing, 1996), p. 3.

11
The Master Key: Choosing Your Words Carefully

The choice to either be fulfilled or destroyed by (his or her) words is given to each person.[1]

— Don Clowers
Minister and Author

In our own lives, we need to see the pattern God used in creating everything and follow that pattern: Idea, choice, action, *words*. Without speaking words in line with, or to carry out the idea you have chosen to put into action, *little if anything will happen.*

Remember: *words are arrows.* Negative words also hit targets, but the wrong targets. The targets hit by negative, doubt-filled, unbelieving words can and will nullify your right choices. Negative words kill; they do not bring life.

Death and life are in the power of the tongue; and they that love it (life) **shall eat the fruit thereof.**

Proverbs 18:21

The Bible calls negative words (words against the promises of God) "perverse speaking."

A wholesome tongue is a tree of life: but perverseness therein is a breach in the spirit.

Proverbs 15:4

There are many other words in the Bible about the importance and the effectiveness, for good or bad, of the words we speak. Following are a few, paraphrased in my own words:

- A good word makes the heart glad (Prov. 12:25).
- Soft words stop anger against you but hard words stir up anger (Prov. 15:1).
- The tongue is a steering wheel that determines the direction of the whole body (James 3:4).
- If you watch your words, you save your life (Prov. 13:3).

Perhaps the strongest warning in the Bible about the consequences of the words we speak is found in Jesus' direct warning in Matthew 12:36,37:

... Every idle word that men shall speak, they shall give account thereof in the day of judgment. For by thy words thou shalt be justified, and by thy words thou shalt be condemned.

"Justified" in that phrase does not imply salvation. Jesus was talking about children of God and the rewards they will receive from the Father when the great reckoning time arrives. Non-believers are condemned because they have not received Jesus as Savior and Lord, not because of their words.

Jesus said in the preceding verses that a good heart was supposed to produce only good words. However, unfortunately, a born-again heart seems capable of producing negative words, words that run counter to the words of Deity as recorded in the Bible.

You can be a Christian and say, "I am one of those persons who comes down with everything that comes along," which is negative speaking and tells your body to receive sickness and disease. You have just hindered your choice to be healthy from hitting its target.

There are cults who think the mind controls the body and sickness is a figment of the imagination. *That is not what I am saying.* There are times when, in spite of choosing to be healthy and in spite of speaking out words from the Bible, you may get sick. However, if this happens, the reason should not be the words of your mouth.

If you "confess" over and over, "I am not sick," when you are, then you are lying. Wisdom dictates accepting the fact that you are sick, *but refusing to accept that sickness has to remain.*

Instead, say, "This sickness has come upon me without my invitation. I do not want it, and I am not going to have it."

Or say, "I'm healed — I just have not received the manifestation yet"; do not say "I'm not sick" when you are. Refuse to keep a headache, do not swear you do not have one.

Denial of Reality Is Not Productive

Denial of true facts does not help you deal with them, nor will it make them go away. Denying that an earthquake has occurred would be obviously silly to anyone. Denying that an "earthquake" has occurred in your life is just as silly and is no way to get rid of it.

Your words have to be, "Okay, the earthquake happened. Now I choose not to let it ruin my life or knock me off the path to my goal. I am going to clean up the mess and go right on."

That kind of response is speaking positive words that will be arrows hitting the target in front of you.

There are many good books available on healing and on how your words and mindset affect health. Get some and read them, as well as read everything in the Bible about health and healing. Set health as your goal, and exercise your right to choose to that end.

There are two things that will stop your positive words, two things that act as a boomerang[2] to cause words to backfire on you. Those two things are unforgiveness and bitterness. (Matt. 18:21,22; Mark 11:25,26; Eph. 4:31; Heb. 12:15, and many others.)

You cannot have unforgiveness and bitterness in your heart toward someone and not think negative thoughts and speak bad words about them. Let go of those feelings if you want to reshape your life, or nothing will reach total fulfillment.

God forgave us much, so we should be willing to forgive others "little" (compared to our sins against Him). Love your enemy, and speak positive words about him. It will amaze you what good that will do in your own life.

Speak positive words (the promises of God) in bad circumstances. In other words, do not choose to agree with circumstances. Instead, choose to agree with the Word of God and be in agreement with the Holy Spirit in order that He may work in your circumstances to turn them for your good and God's glory.

Reality is that sometimes achieving one's goals does not happen overnight. It is not easy to continue to speak positive words when the road goes on and on, and you never seem to get to the goal.

Reality is that adults on the road to prosperity, happiness, and fulfilled goals are sometimes like small children riding in the back of the car with mom and dad on a long trip. We ask over and over again how soon will we get there and how long will it be. We want to give up and go back home. We get tired, discouraged, and lose hope.

We look at time instead of goals, like the children asking the same questions every five minutes: Are we there yet? The Apostle Paul warned us not "to get weary in well-doing."

(Gal. 6:9.) If we keep on keeping on, "in due season," we will win the prize, reach the goal, accomplish our purposes, Paul wrote.

Nineteenth-century author Charles Buxton put this aspect of life very succinctly:

> The road to success is not to be run upon by seven-league boots. Step by step, little by little, bit by bit, that is the way to wealth, that is the way to wisdom, that is the way to glory.[3]

Your happiness does not have to depend on reaching the goal. In other words, you can be happy along the way to the goal. It does not have to be deferred. Happiness, like almost everything else in our lives, is the result of a choice.

---

[1]Clowers, Don. *Spiritual Growth*, (Dallas: Don Clowers Ministries, Inc., production by Image Source, Tulsa, OK, 1995), p. 59.

[2]A "boomerang" is a native Australian weapon designed to be thrown and automatically rebound to the one who threw it.

[3]*New Dictionary of Thoughts*, (Standard Book Company, 1965), "Success," p. 645, Charles Buxton (1823-1871.)

12
How To Choose Happiness

The world of the happy is quite another than the world of the unhappy.[1]

— Ludwig Wittgenstein
German Philosopher

Most of us let events, other people, and circumstances control our happiness. We blame those things instead of exercising personal authority.

People who have been victorious in life are those who have discovered this fact. Begin with the Apostle Paul, who wrote that in spite of beatings, prison, hunger and thirst, and ill health, he had learned to be happy.

> **But I rejoiced in the Lord greatly, that now at the last your care of me hath flourished again; . . . Not that I speak in respect of want: for I have learned, in whatsoever state I am, therewith to be content.**
> **Philippians 4:10,11**

Somehow, we usually think that meant he had become resigned to his ministry assignment, that he had learned not to complain in hard times, that he was stoical, long-suffering, and waiting to be happy in Heaven. However, Paul wrote that he had learned to be *content*.

What does *content* mean? The Greek adjective translated "content" in the New Testament is *autarkes*, which originally meant "sufficient in oneself," which includes not needing someone or something else to make one happy.[2] The English words listed in a thesaurus as meaning the same as "to be contented" are:

> Satisfied, *happy*, pleased, comfortable, at ease, carefree, fulfilled, serene, tranquil . . . .[3]

Nowhere in any dictionary or thesaurus will you find the definition of *content* listed as "long-suffering, resigned to one's fate, 'hunkered-down' under the winds of trouble, gritting-one's-teeth-and-bearing-it."

No! The truth is that Paul learned he could *choose to be happy*. The basis of his choice to be happy was his previous choice, and total commitment, to reach the goal for his life that God intended: to take the good news of Jesus to the non-Jewish world.

You will find it is possible to choose each day to be happy once you choose to believe that God loves you and that circumstances may control your movements, but only you can control your thinking.

When you allow events, circumstances, and other people to control your happiness, you are voluntarily giving those things authority over your life.

If someone does something bad to you, choose to forgive and be happy anyway. Otherwise, you are allowing that person to add insult to injury. You are in essence "cutting off your own nose to spite your face."

One wise man has written that, since the technological revolution:

> No longer can man blame something outside of himself.
> Man must blame himself.
> Man does what he does because he chooses thus to do.[4]

Happiness Begins With You

However, there is no way you can choose happiness if you do not like yourself. The butcher in the story in a previous chapter who was going broke obviously did not like himself. He thought of himself as a failure; therefore, he was making choices to fulfill that expectation.

This is why any changes in your life must begin with your personality, your attitudes, and your own behavior.

South African evangelist/pastor Norman Robertson says, "The me I see is the me I'll be."[5]

That is not a cliche or a motivational saying. It is a fact of life.

Albert Einstein did not see himself as retarded or slow to learn, although he was called that in school. The "me" he saw in himself was the genius the world eventually saw.

Who is the "me" you see in the mirror every morning? You will find yourself more able to hold onto that positive image all through the day if you take a few minutes every morning to take authority over your thoughts and plan your day. Even if it means getting up 15 minutes early, you will find it well worth the loss of that much sleep.

This period of setting goals for your day should include prayer, planning short-term goals (things to be accomplished this day), and making quality choices, beginning with these:

- I choose to be happy today.
- I choose to do everything I do today as unto the Lord.
- I choose to achieve my short-term goals today.
- I choose to use this day to good advantage toward my long-term goals.

- I choose to be a conqueror today and not a pretender nor one who fritters time away on fantasies (ideas with no plans to work them out).

British statesman Edmund Burke wrote:

> The great difference between the real (conqueror) and the pretender is that the one sees into the future, while the other regards only the present; the one lives by the day and acts on expediency; the other acts on enduring principles and for immortality.[6]

I pray that everyone who has read this book has experienced a great light going off in mind and heart, so to speak, and will begin to take charge of his or her life.

---

[1]Wittgenstein, Ludwig. *Tractatus Logico-Philosophicus* (1922), *The Oxford Dictionary of Quotations*, 3rd ed., p. 575.16.

[2]Vine, W.E. *Vine's Expository Dictionary of Old and New Testament Words*, (Old Tappan, N.J.: Fleming H. Revell Company, 1981), Vol. I, p. 234.

[3]McCutcheon, Marc, editor. *Roget's Super Thesaurus*, (Cincinnati: Writer's Digest Books, 1991, 1st ed.), p. 118.

[4]Kohe, p. 58.

[5]Robertson, Norman. *Winners in Christ*, (Charlotte, N.C.: NRM Publications, 1995), p. 27.

[6]*The New Dictionary of Thoughts*, p. 407.

13
Bad Things Happen When Good Men Do Nothing

A worldview is the culturally determined set of filters through which we perceive and experience reality.[1]

— Zeb Long and Douglas McMurry
Missionary-Evangelists, Pastors, Authors

Once you begin to exercise your right to choose with the purpose of conforming to the image of Jesus, obviously your new choices and your conformed personality and life will affect the lives of your family, your friends, and the people with whom you work. However, there is a dimension beyond that: Your choices can have an effect on society as well.

Particularly as an American citizen, you have a responsibility to make choices in government and society that will cause God's Kingdom "to come on earth as it is in Heaven." (Matt. 6:10.)

The first battle the Nazis won was when the people who saw the evil aims of Hitler's regime did nothing to stop them —

Christian and non-Christian alike. "Good" people did nothing in Germany (or around the world for months and months), consequently, extremely "bad" things happened.

As a speaker, professional businessman, and author, I would be remiss in carrying out my assignment to show other Christians how to receive the blessings that are theirs under the New Covenant (Gal. 3:26-29) if I ended this book only with how their choices affect themselves. No one goes through life without his or her choices having an effect on others and on society in general.

In terms of government, exercising your right to choose in the United States first of all means choosing to register to vote, then choosing to vote. To vote according to the will of God, you must make the effort to be well informed on the issues involved and about the candidates on the ballot.

After you understand the issues and know as much as you can about the candidates' positions, then you pray for guidance as to how to vote. Only God knows men's hearts. (1 Kings 8:39; Luke 16:15.) Candidates have been known to campaign as statesmen but turn into politicians once in office!

Some Christians may feel led by their consciences and even by the witness of the Holy Spirit to run for office. If this "call" comes to you, then you have the chance to choose whether to serve God in this way. Israel's wisest king wrote:

> **When the righteous are in authority,**
> **the people rejoice;**
>
> **But when a wicked man rules,**
> **the people groan.**
>
> **Proverbs 29:2 NKJV**

In addition, part of being a "rightstanding" citizen of the Kingdom of God on earth is to pray for those who are in office, even if you did not vote for them, like them personally, or agree with everything they do.

> **I urge then, first of all, that requests, prayers, intercession and thanksgiving, be made for everyone — for kings and all those in authority, that we may live peaceful and quiet lives in all godliness and holiness.**
>
> **1 Timothy 2:1,2**

As I said in an earlier chapter, our choices are not made in a vacuum. Without effort and without establishing a practice of checking everything by the Word of God and by the character of Jesus, our choices in any area will be "slanted" toward the world's philosophy and not in true alignment with God's will and our knowledge of Him.

The Apostle Paul warned the early Christians about the dangers of getting off-base in following Jesus through following the thinking or the worldview of the secular society of his day.

> **Beware lest anyone cheat you through philosophy and empty deceit, according to the tradition of men, according to the basic principles of the world, and not according to Christ.**
>
> **Colossians 2:8 NKJV**

Why did Paul use the word *cheat*? He used it because that is exactly what knowledge based on anti-biblical principles does: it cheats you of a right-thinking mind. The NIV translation says:

> **See to it that no one takes you captive through hollow and deceptive philosophy which depends on human tradition and the basic principles of this world rather than on Christ.**

Both translations make it plain that Paul knew philosophy or a worldview based on human tradition not only can cheat you of peace and happiness but may even put you in mental bondage.

The world's philosophy and much of its education always has amounted to a foundation of "sand," not bedrock.

Without Jesus in your life, your "house is built on sand." (Matt. 7:24-27.)

Without Bible-based systems, society, cultures, and governments are built on sand.

Most major Christian writers define the United States and most of the entire western world as primarily "pagan," and no longer a Judeo-Christian culture and society. This did not happen overnight or without the Body of Christ allowing it through doing nothing at the very least, or by choosing the wisdom of the world at the most.

During the half-century since World War II, a majority of "good men" and women have exercised their rights to choose to "do nothing" about the downward trend of thinking in society. (Any trend away from God and biblical morality is "downward.") The Church has not fulfilled its responsibility to choose (seek) first the Kingdom of God. (Matt. 6:33.)

Long and McMurry wrote:

> God has a will of His own, a way of doing the very thing we insist He cannot or will not do. . . . We must, like Jesus, learn to see what God is doing and then align ourselves with it.[2]

How can we be sure we are using our God-given inalienable right to choose in line with Kingdom principles?

We do this by examining the way we see the world — science, government, education, culture, and so forth — and then adjusting our thinking to what the Bible tells us is true in those areas.

Changing Your "Filter"

You may say, "But the Bible is not a scientific book. It does not tell us how atoms are split or how sheep can be cloned."

No, God did not see fit to fill us in on all the details of His creation or the creative process. However, if any scientific principles contradict the Word of God, then we can choose not to believe them.

- *Do we choose to believe God created the earth and everything in it, including mankind? Or do we choose to buy into the world's philosophy that man and animals evolved from a common ancestor but no one knows exactly how it came into being?*

The first choice puts us on a path to becoming sons and daughters of the Creator, members of a new race born again through Jesus, God's only begotten Son. (John 3:16.)

The second choice causes us to believe all life, human or animal, is equal in value and importance, that awareness ends with the death of the body, and that Tarzan's "ape-foster mother" is equal to a loving, kind human mother and her death just as much to be mourned as a loving human mother, a logical extension of thought based on the theory of evolution.[3]

The first choice causes us to value the life of an unborn child as much as one already born; the second choice causes us to view unborn humans as no more than animals to be discarded at will.

- *Do we choose to believe the wisdom of the Bible as to the real basis of "life, liberty, and the pursuit of happiness"? Or do we choose to believe psychology, all of the "self-actualization" theories, schemes, and plans so popular over the past two decades?*

C. S. Lewis made the observation that God designed mankind like an automaker designs a gasoline engine. It will not run on any fuel but gasoline, without being modified into a different kind of machine. God designed man to run on Himself, and there is no real happiness in life if our choices are aimed at running on another kind of fuel: pride, fear, false religions, atheism, or philosophies that make man his own god.

> That is the key to history. Terrific energy is expended — civilizations are built up — excellent institutions devised, but each time something goes wrong. Some fatal flaw always brings the selfish and cruel people to the top, and it all slides back into misery and ruin.[4]

- *Do we believe that morality is based on the "Thou shalt nots" of the law given to Moses?* (Ex. 20.) *Or do we believe "morality" is based on situations and circumstances?*

For the past forty years, the second belief has become more and more prevalent. The result is the "paganization" of the West. Ralph Waldo Emerson penned a short poem about great men that sums up what right choices of individuals can do to mold and change civilization.

> Not gold, but only men can make
>   A people great and strong;
>
> Men who, for truth and honor's sake,
>   Stand fast and suffer long.
>
> Brave men who work while others sleep,
>   Who dare while others fly —
>
> They build a nation's pillars deep
>   And lift them to the sky.[5]

For Such a Time as This

America's "pillars" were deep and lifted to the sky from the first settlers to the moon landing. When the majority of Americans' choices began to be to "separate church and state" (even the choices of many Christians who should have known better), the the pillars began to rock and our height and greatness began to crumble.

The ancient teller of fables, Aesop, said, "Real bravery lies in deeds, not words."[6]

To paraphrase that thought, let me say that "real change in your life or in society lies in right choices, not in lackadaisical acceptance of the status quo."

Even those brought up in Christian, church-going families and educated in Christian schools can have their "filters" contaminated by all of the ungodly television programs, movies, and publications, as well as the lyrics of the music that bombards us wherever we go.

Therefore, my thoughts on "your greatest asset" would not be complete without the warning that your worldview, the "filter" through which you decide what is true or untrue around you, periodically needs cleansing. Even after you have checked everything you believe by the Bible as the Bereans did in New Testament days (Acts 17:11), you should know that "dust and debris" from what you see and hear each day will "clog up" your view of events, issues, and how to behave. Then you could be "cheated" of your birthright: your right to choose.

Not being conned into making the wrong choices is important in anyone's life and in any society, nation, or culture. However, looking at history, one can see that some points in time are more strategic than others. Enough right choices in the late 30s in Germany, for instance, could have saved millions of lives. That point marked a turning point in the history of the world. No nation or civilization has been the same since.

In the book of Esther, the Bible relates a time in ancient history that correlates with Nazi Germany. Through the choice of an evil man, Haman, the Jewish nation in exile in Persia almost suffered the fate of Jews living in Germany in the early 40s. It is possible, you see, that one man's choice in manipulation of events can change history.

The king of Persia at the time, however, had just taken a Jewish girl as queen. (Read the entire book. It is a fascinating story.) Her cousin, Mordecai, who had reared her, exercised his inalienable right to choose to ask her to intercede with the king, although it could have meant losing her life to do so.

His words to her essentially formed a question I would like to ask every reader of this book: who knows but what you were born for such a time as this? (Esther 4:14.)

I would like to end with a couple of verses that illustrate the biggest enemy of your inalienable right: procrastination.

> Mr. Meant-To has a comrade,
>   And his name is Didn't-Do,
>
> Have you ever chanced to meet them?
>   Did they ever call on you?
>
> These two fellows live together
>   In the house of Never-Win,
>
> And I'm told that it is haunted
>   By the ghost of Might-Have-Been.[7]

Benjamin Franklin, the statesman I have used as an example of someone who not only set a goal of choosing to change, but actually changed his personality with the help of God, once wrote:

> Work while it is called today, for you know how much you may be hindered tomorrow. One today is worth two tomorrows, never leave that till tomorrow which you can do today.[8]

---

[1] Long, Zeb Bradford and McMurry, Douglas. *The Collapse of the Brass Heaven*, (Grand Rapids: Chosen Books, Baker Book House, 1994), p. 26.

[2] Ibid, pp. 218, 219.

[3] Author's Note: See the ending of the movie, *Greystoke*, a modern version of Edgar Rice Burrough's classic series about Tarzan, a fictional boy supposed to have been reared by apes in the African jungles.

[4] Lewis, *Mere Christianity*, p. 54.

[5] Bennett, William J. *The Book of Virtues*, (New York: Simon & Schuster, 1993), p. 418.

[6] Ibid, p. 457.

[7] Ibid, p. 364.

[8] Ibid.

Ten Life-Changing Choices

Choose Jesus as Savior and Lord, which means you have chosen Heaven as your final destination and God as your Father.

Choose to accept the responsibility for exercising the one inalienable right God has given you: the right to choose!

Choose a confident life, not a timid one.

Choose a happy life, not unhappiness or discontentment.

Choose to have a peaceful spirit, not a restless one.

Choose a calm mind; choose rest in the Lord, not confusion.

Choose getting along with others, not contentiousness.

Choose to make the most of your life, not be defeated.

Choose goals to make your life what you want it to be.

Choose prosperity, not poverty.

To quote Daniels once again:

By now, you may have realized that you do possess a powerful "magic wand"; it is called "choice," and it is waiting for you to "press the button" called *decision* (your will) to make the required adjustments in your life.[1]

And I say "amen" to that!

---

[1] Daniels, p. 51.

About the Author

Tom Leding is a noted Tulsa businessman, broadcaster, and author who has touched the lives of thousands with his motivational messages for success in life.

The Clarksville, Arkansas, native earned bachelor's degrees in accounting and business law from the Oklahoma School of Business and LaSalle University, plus a master's degree in business administration from Golden State University. Additional years of study paid off with a doctorate from the University of Hawaii.

He was chief accountant at American Airlines for nearly five years.

For twenty-three years he was an agent with the Farmer's Insurance Group, where he set company records for the largest single policy ever sold as well as monthly and annual sales marks. For seven years he was Number One among the company's fourteen thousand agents.

Today, Tom has ten brokers working in his full-service insurance and investment agency, while he personally manages a multimillion dollar portfolio for his clients.

His daily radio and television broadcasts called, "Who Said That?" inspire listeners to reach beyond their present circumstances to be the best they can be. He has appeared on the Christian Broadcasting Network and the Trinity Broadcasting Network and also is in demand as a motivational speaker across the country.

Called the "Man with the Midas Touch" by *Voice Magazine*, Tom is the author of the bestselling books *Who Said That?*, *Rags to Riches: You Don't Have To Be Poor*, *The Making of a King: You Can Rise Above Your Circumstances*, and *The Leding Action Plan for Success*. Antioch Christian University recently awarded Tom an Honorary Doctor of Literature Degree in recognition of his contribution to Christian literature.

A member of the Full Gospel Business Men's Fellowship since 1955, Tom is International Treasurer of the fellowship, which has more than 4,000 chapters in 150 nations. Within six months of his appointment as Vice President for Membership, the Tulsa FGBMFI Chapter became the fastest growing chapter in the nation.

He also has served on the boards of Kenneth Hagin Ministries, Youth for Christ and other ministries.

Tom and his wife, Sue, have one son, Ron, and two grandchildren. Sue and Ron are both licensed agents.

Other titles by Tom Leding

Rags to Riches: You Don't Have To Be Poor offers practical steps you can take to break out of the bonds of poverty and walk in your inheritance as a child of God. $10.

Wisdom for Success in Life will inspire you to escape the ordinary and be the best you can be. $10. Also available as an audio book for $20.

The Making of a King: You Can Rise Above Your Circumstances details nearly forty things you must have, do, be, or achieve to "reign" in your chosen field. Failure will never overtake you if your determination to succeed is strong enough. $15.

The Leding Action Plan for Success guides you step by step in how to discover and implement God's plan for your life. $10.

To order, call:
1-800-880-8220

Or write to:

TLM Publishing
4412 S. Harvard
Tulsa, OK 74135